HOW TO MEDITATE IN JUST 2 MINUTES:

Easy Meditation & Stress Relief for Beginners and Experts Alike

***** *"A terrific resource and guide for anyone seeking information and tips on meditating."*
- ReadersFavorite.com

"I'm a convert and I'm spreading the word on this little gem of a book."
- Keith Williams, Psychotherapist & Author

PHIL PIERCE

What Can You Get From This Book?

- Do you know the 'trick' to relax anywhere?

- How to unlock your brain's secret potential?

- How to choose the right way to relax (unique to you)?

- 7 effective (and different) methods for Meditation

- Practical exercises anyone can do

- Do you know the best body position for your meditation?

- How to quiet your mind?

- The amazing benefits of Mindfulness

- The 2 Minute Secret

- The biggest 'Mistake' most people make

And more

The simple aim of this book is to give you powerful and practical tips for a more relaxed and focused body and mind.

This down-to-earth, no-nonsense approach is perfect for beginners and experts alike. With methods to help you boost energy, increase mindfulness and discover a healthier lifestyle all through easy-to-follow meditation and relaxation tactics

(And reveal some little-known secrets about the incredible benefits Meditation can offer!)

Ever wondered how to 'switch off' and 'tune in'? You may be surprised how easy it is…

Contents

How to Use this Guide (A foreword)

The practical techniques in this guide are powerful, effective and easily achieved but a word of advice;

You don't need to rush into it!

While you can jump in and 'have a go' the very best results are always found from a deeper understanding of the Meditation and Mindfulness process as a whole. (As described throughout this book.)

We live in times of instant gratification, where whatever we need can be had faster and easier than ever before.

Hungry? Go to a vending machine or fast food outlet
Need to know something? The internet has the answer in seconds.

Because of this we have become programmed to look for the quickest route to what we desire, but this isn't always the *best* route. In taking that shortcut or skipping the journey we often miss a vital part of the experience.

The same is true with meditation.

For many, the temptation with this guide will be to skip straight to the practical chapters and dive right into the physical part of "How to Meditate".

There is nothing wrong with this of course. You will still gain a benefit from understanding how to perform correct positions and mindfulness in general but without the surrounding understanding of *why* you will really only get half of the story.

It is only in understanding the reasons behind our actions and the benefits they have that we create a powerful and long-lasting routine, especially in the case of Meditation.

So take your time, enjoy the learning process and, in doing so, gain a full and deeper understanding of not just meditation but also yourself. If anything, this is the first lesson.

From The Author

Take a breath; now hold it for a couple of seconds and exhale. Feeling more relaxed?

You've just started on the path to a better, more relaxed and healthy lifestyle and you've already taken the first step in reading this book.

The aim of this simple guide is to give you the tips and techniques for daily life allowing you to make the most of your mind and body in easy to follow short routines that anyone can do. (Because most of us don't have time to visit a remote retreat or consult a Zen master).

The approach here is one of jargon-free explanation for the everyman/woman because meditation should be for everyone, not an exclusive elite few hidden halfway up a mountain!

While you might ultimately be seeking spiritual Nirvana or ascension to some higher plane of consciousness it is important to start small and focus on developing a realistic approach to relaxation. This book helps you establish a set of easy-to-do, easy-to-maintain and uncomplicated exercises that are perfect for the overstressed office worker, busy mother, exhausted manager or anyone in-between.

Over the years I have been lucky enough to train around the world in Martial Arts but also numerous styles of relaxation and body awareness exercises, including forms of Tai Chi, Meditation and Qi Gong. One thing I have witnessed in all of these is the benefits of regular practice.

We start small though because studies have shown that the real benefits of meditation are found with regularity. A short 2-minute exercise maintained every day is incredibly easy to follow and yields fantastic results. Anything longer or more intense can be too much for the average person to stick to, which is no criticism of the individual, simply an observation on the intensely busy lives we lead in the modern world.

Grabbing a quiet two minutes whenever you can will help focus your mind and regenerate your body.

If you are solely focused on the practical exercises then feel free to skip straight to the sections regarding the 2 minute meditation practice and the principals of relaxation – after all this is a guide, not an instruction – but I encourage reading the surrounding sections also for a deeper understanding of the principals these exercises are built on.

I hope you find this book helpful.

- *Phil*

The Exercises

Throughout this book and at the end of each section you will see exercises that you can complete. These are designed to not only introduce you to a number of new meditation techniques but also help you get into the habit of establishing a meditation practice.

There are a number of different ideas and techniques to help you find which ones work for you but if like me, you prefer to read a whole book before diving into the practical aspects, that's fine too.

At the end, I've collated all the exercises into a few pages, so you can start at the beginning and really get a feel for what meditation can do for you.

If you don't want to do the exercises, that's fine too of course, but you will be missing out on a huge part of learning the amazing benefits a small amount of mindfulness can bring.

If you really want to make a change for the better and improve your physical and mental well-being, there is no better way than meditation…but you do have to take action. Unlike many methods, two-minute meditation is quick and effective but you still have to commit to that small amount of time and the actions required.

Many people reading this guide will simply skim through the exercises, never take action and never discover a calmer, more focused mind. Will that be you? Or will you be one of the success stories?

It's in your hands.

The 2 Minute Secret

Keeping it Simple

There are hundreds of Meditation guides out there. You probably saw a few of them before looking here, and most of them focus on learning long intense meditations for achieving inner enlightenment.

There is of course nothing wrong with this. Indeed seeking spiritual enlightenment is a noble goal, but most of these guides fail to address the fact that as humans we are incredibly lazy.

Not that we can't be bothered to get up off the couch (although that can be the case!), but that our brains are wired to take the shortest and easiest route to a target.

Cognitive Laziness – if you will.

It's this instinct that means by default we will subconsciously not act upon something unless it is life or death. (Or requires little to no resistance)

Unfortunately, willpower alone is a poor motivator for most people.

So despite the proven benefits of meditation, it is estimated that a tiny percentage of people around the world regularly practice it.

It's a bit like fitness and exercise in this regard. Most people know it is good for them so why don't they do it?

Typically two reasons/excuses present themselves:

Lack of time

And/or

Lack of Knowing How

Time Investment

With regards to a lifestyle investment, many people perceive Meditation practice as a time-consuming exercise requiring hours and hours of practice every week but this simply isn't true.

"I don't have the time" many say. *"I'm too busy"*.

The first notion to dispel is that meditation requires many hours before any results are seen. The truth is that in just 2 minutes of quiet focus you can achieve the same physical and mental benefits as in a 10, 15 or 30-minute session.

Sure, longer durations CAN be more beneficial, increasing the therapeutic time, but not necessarily. It's far better to meditate daily for only 2 minutes than once a week for 15 minutes. Similarly, 2 minutes of quiet focus and mindfulness are hugely superior to spending 10 minutes of restless fidgeting trying to achieve the Lotus position.

The moral of the story?

Quality not Quantity

And

Regularity not Duration

Know How

The second most commonly touted obstacle to Meditation practice is a lack of knowledge or not knowing what to do.

This typically occurs in people that have either attempted meditation once and given up or those that have never attempted it and use this as a reason not to.

The fact is that meditation doesn't require much in the way of training or expert know-how because we are instinctively programmed to be mindful and aware of our own body anyway. We just need to let it happen.

Ironically we are usually the ones to blame for over complicating things in our own life.

Long Meditation training courses and tutorials are often pointless because all we need is a little guidance to shut off external distractions and return to our most natural state of self-awareness.

That's not to say some extra knowledge won't help, but for many, the obsession with learning everything about meditation really just masks a fear of getting started.

A short guide (like this) and the will to act is all you need to begin...

The Truth

But a lack of time and/or know-how is not really the issue with many people. If we dig a little deeper we see that priorities are.

If 2 Minutes of work could win you the lottery you can bet you would suddenly find the time and the knowledge to give it a go.

And yet the benefits of Meditation are akin to winning the lottery in many respects; reduced risk of heart disease, reduced stress and even longer life are all attributed to its practice.

Indeed there have been over 1000 documented studies of meditation showing scientifically proven benefits including:

- Lower Risk of Heart Attack or Stroke (Up to 15%)
- Insomnia reduction (75% of sufferers saw improvement in sleep)
- Anxiety reduction (60% of people showed improvement)

And much more. (See 'The Benefits of Meditation' later in this guide)

Did you know according to a recent Nielsen study the average American spends approximately 34 Hours A WEEK, watching TV? That's a full day and a half spent staring at the Television!

We all love a bit of film and entertainment so it's natural to spend time enjoying this but at 34 hours a week, it's not just a waste of time but outright unhealthy!

Yet we do it because it's easy; it triggers no resistance from our conscience.

Meditation, Exercise or any activity requiring some perceived effort has to overcome this mental desire to do as little as possible.

So the trick is to 'hack' our brains into accepting a short but regular meditation routine.

"Just 2 minutes"

Consider these words anytime you need motivation.

The 2 Minute approach is a bite-size, easily digestible approach to Meditation offering all of the benefits for a tiny outlay of time.

2 Minutes is nothing. It takes longer to make a coffee. Anyone can manage 2 minutes and so can you.

(For an extra helping hand also check out 'Quick Tips and Tricks' later in this guide)

Any trigger can signal the time to begin a meditation and since the 2 Minute approach is a short duration you can be finished before you need to move onto something else.

- During an ad break on TV
- While the kettle boils
- Before bed
- When waking up.

All of these are perfect signals to tune out from your chaotic life for just 2 minutes. And as you get better at the process, you will find that even in this relatively short space of time you are able to fully switch off and quiet your thoughts, achieving the benefits of a longer meditation but in a quicker, manageable format.

Consider this. A total of 14 Minutes of Meditation a week to help focus, relaxation and overall health.

Or

A total of 2040 Minutes a week of T.V. to .... Sorry, I've got nothing.

EXERCISE ONE:

Set a timer on your phone or computer for two minutes, with an alarm at the end. Start the countdown and then go back to whatever you were doing in your daily life. Don't look at the timer.

Whether you were at work, on the computer or out walking—whatever you were up to I guarantee that the alarm will go off quicker than expected. Two minutes feels like nothing at all.

Still feel like you don't have the time to spare?

"I have so much to accomplish today that I must meditate for two hours instead of one".

-   *Gandhi*

How to Begin: The 2 Minute Process

Meditation is always a personal experience and you are encouraged to approach it in whatever way is most comfortable to you. After reading through this guide you may find some techniques resonate more with you than others which is to be expected.

Once you have a preferred method you can incorporate this into your daily practice or regular schedule. But before you get to that point you may wish to begin with the most simple of the approaches: *2 Minute Breathing.*

Focused breathing forms the basis for the majority of all Meditation and Mindfulness exercises and so if you can perfect this you can easily move onto longer durations or other techniques.

The following breaks the process down into 30-second segments to further aid in structuring your approach. As always this is just a guide that can be modified as you see fit:

0-30 Seconds
- **Becoming Quiet and Still**

To start, your body and mind may be unsettled as you enter into the meditation. Use this first 30 seconds to do your best to become still and calm in both. Focus on staying in one position (of your choice) and slowing your thoughts. You may close your eyes to help this.

30-60 Seconds
- **Focus on the Breath**

Next, draw your attention to your breathing. Begin inhaling through your nose and out through your mouth. Focus fully on each breath and inhale for a mental count of 5, hold for a count of 2 and exhale for a count of 5. Then repeat.

60-90 Seconds
- **Expand Your Awareness**

Now allow your thoughts to expand and fully acknowledge your own body and all of its sensations. Don't judge or try to change anything. Allow your mind to be free of concern and become loosely aware of how that feels.

90-120 Seconds
-   **Combine and Close**

With all the previous parts combined; stillness, focused breathing and a relaxed expanded awareness, you should find you feel calm and yet alert, focused and yet thought-free.

It is at this point where all the elements coalesce that you find the most power; a kind of therapeutic trance state which is almost impossible to put into words. (And feels completely unique for you so you don't need to try!)

Finally, as the time draws to a close take some deeper breaths and draw your attention to the ground, chair or cushion on which you sit. Feel and listen for your physical surroundings and when you are ready to open your eyes.

Don't Worry if it Doesn't Happen Right Away

The process above is the ideal way a brief 2 Minute meditation will play out but if it doesn't happen that way for you there is nothing to worry about.

It's very common for the process to be as different as the individual practicing it. Simply use each 30-second strategy as a guide if you find your thoughts wandering, to bring them back in line.

Eventually, you will find the process becomes second nature and you won't even need to think about it. The same approach can also be applied to longer sessions in the same way but for different durations.

What can Meditation do for Me?

The Personal Journey

If you are reading this book chances are you already have a rough idea about the benefits of Meditation and even if you aren't sure there is a good chance you have heard about it through friends, family or popular media.

But here's the problem:

None of those things matter. Not really.

Meditation is one of the most personal experiences an individual can go through and entering it with expectations of achieving or feeling what others have is very tricky.

Your brain is totally unique. Every thought and feeling you have is your own and shaped to you. Hence it's really impossible to say what everyone will achieve in Meditation or how they will react.

Imagine trying to describe the color Blue to someone. Or the smell of the ocean. Our interpretation of the world around us is entirely shaped by our own perception and so trying to impart that to someone else is nearly impossible.

Instead, try to open yourself to be fully accepting of whatever you feel when you start to Meditate. Once we let go of our preconceptions and expectations a whole new world of experience is there for us. One that is not colored by anything other than the moment we are in.

This is the start of mindfulness, being in the present.

What can you expect?

While it is impossible to truly predict how you will feel and respond to Meditation there are a number of beneficial feelings and bodily reactions that are most commonly experienced by most people. Including:

- Improved Sleep
- Reduced Stress
- Increased Focus
- Lower Blood pressure

- Better tolerance of those around you
- Improved resistance to illness
- Improved awareness
- Increased Brain function
- Reduced Cognitive decline
- And much more

EXERCISE TWO:

What do you want to achieve from meditation? There is no right or wrong answer to this question but you do need to think about it.

Take a notepad or create a note on your phone and write down:

- Three things that stress you out on a regular basis
- Three ways you would like to improve this
- Three things you would like to get from meditation – your goals.

Where does Meditation Come from?

The origins of meditation are closely tied to religion. During the prehistoric age, societies used a practice akin to meditation in an effort to satisfy their gods. This ritual included repeated chants vocalized in rhythm. Academics theorize that meditation may have played a significant role in the evolutionary progress of increased focal abilities in the later stages of human development.

The Bible also holds indications of meditation being practiced as early as 1400 BCE. Accounts in the Vedas from the Hindu religion trace meditation to that time as well while a more established form of meditation is seen in China within the Taoist religion and in India's Buddhism during the sixth and fifth centuries.

Traveling towards the west in Alexandria, Philo is credited with writing about "spiritual exercises" in 20 BCE. These required both concentration and "prosoche", or attention. Later, in the third century, Plotinus would create specific meditation techniques.

In the first century BCE, the Pāli Canon put further emphasis on India's Buddhist meditation, deeming the practice an act which could lead an individual closer to salvation. Around that same time, China was being introduced to Buddhism. A text known as the Vimalakirti Sutra from 100 CE holds multiple passages referring to meditation as one of the major pathways to achieving Zen. Through trade routes nicknamed the Silk Road, Buddhism and meditation, in general, continued to spread

In approximately 1227 Dōgen returned from China and inscribed the guidelines for Zazen or seated meditation. In the eighth or ninth century, Islam's Dhikr practice adopted a repetitive exercise including 99 terms for God. Another religious connection involved Sufism which, as early as the twelfth century had developed meditation techniques including breath work and repeated holy terms.

Though unproven, it is likely that contact with the Sufis and or Indians catalyzed the meditative nature with which Eastern Christianity developed hesychasm or experiential prayer. The practice of hesychasm sprouted somewhere between the 10th and 14th centuries upon Mount Athos in Greece. It includes repeated recitation of the Jesus Prayer.

One of the big differences which sets the meditation used in Western Christianity apart from that of Eastern Christianity is the absence of repeated phrases or actions. It also lacks a specified posture. This meditation has been developed from Lectio Divina, which can be translated to divine reading, or in this case bible reading. This practice was the primary focus of the Benedictine monks during the sixth century. During the 12th century, a monk named   Guigo II established the four formal steps of Lectio Divina, arranged on a conceptual ladder. These included lectio, meditatio, oratio, and contemplatio. Translated they are reading, pondering, praying, and contemplation, respectively.

Another advancement of meditation within Western Christianity is traced to various saints including Ignatius of Loyola and Teresa of Avila during the 16th century. During the 1700's Buddhism gained the attention of western scholars. One, in particular, was the popular philosopher, Schopenhauer. Meanwhile, Voltaire requested that communities approach Buddhists with tolerance.

1927 saw the first translation of the Tibetan Book of the Dead into the English language. Further on, in the 1950's India was introduced to new secular meditation practices. In the following decade, Europe and the United States were greeted with Hindu meditation practices which had developed a more westernized approach. In this version, the focus shifted from spiritual growth to relaxation, self-improvement, and stress relief.

The original and westernized mediation practices have since undergone inspection by the scientific community. Though the first studies were initiated in 1931, interest in such exploration has increased greatly since the 1970's. In fact, following that particular surge over 1000 meditation studies have been recorded in English alone.

Unlock Your Brain's Secret Potential: The Incredible Scientific Discoveries Behind Meditation

What is going on in <u>your</u> mind?

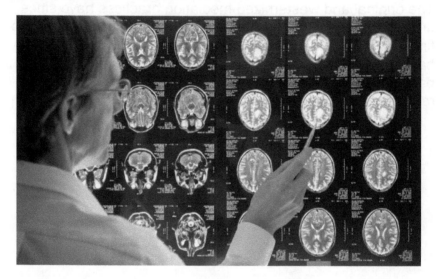

Meditation in various forms has been practiced for millennia, but it's only recently with the advances in medicine, science and technology that we are finally understanding exactly what it is doing to our brain and body. Some of the results are amazing...

Buddhists have practiced meditation for more than five thousand years. This has offered plenty of time for them to witness its benefits. Many have seen personal identities growing stronger. Thoughts have become more insightful. And their spiritual devotion developing deeper roots.

Some theorize that the meditation practiced by the monks of Buddhism is similar to the prayers utilized in Christianity. Both typically involve sitting quietly and focusing the mind on a special task. The largest and most profound difference is that while one who prays attempts to access God, one who meditates seeks to channel the power of their own mind within.

In more modern times, meditation has begun to breach the borders of religion. You no longer need to be a Buddhist in order to reap its benefits. Today meditation is seen as both an ancient spiritual practice, and a modern tool for obtaining greater mental and physical health.

Practicing Meditation Transforms Your Brain

Neuroscientists have begun studying the merits of meditation in a more scientific manner than ever before. The development of the MRI and other scanning methods for viewing the brain have changed the way medical professionals view the practice. Once cast off, as a purely psychological event, we can now clearly see that meditation does, in fact, alter the brain in a positive way.

Thanks to important research, it is now believed that meditation can prove advantageous when used as a therapeutic aid in the treatment of numerous clinical disorders, not limited to epilepsy, depression, insomnia, or anxiety.

While its initial use was based purely on perceived benefits, science is now beginning to confirm its validity through observed changes in the chemical and electrical activities of the brain.

Curious as to which regions of the brain were involved in meditation, researchers of the Harvard Medical School used the MRI to observe the brains of meditating participants. Their studies revealed that the areas affected were from the region governing the autonomic nervous system. This area controls involuntary actions like blood pressure and digestion. Because this area is vulnerable to negative stress, it makes sense that an activity, which stimulates this region, would be effective at preventing stress-related ailments like infertility, heart disease, or digestive disorders.

The transformations that meditation causes within the brain can be divided into two broad categories. The first category includes physical or chemical changes while the second focuses on alterations in the way the brain functions.

Physical and Chemical Changes

Neuroscientists have used MRI imaging to show that meditation can strengthen an individual's brain through redefining important brain cell connections.

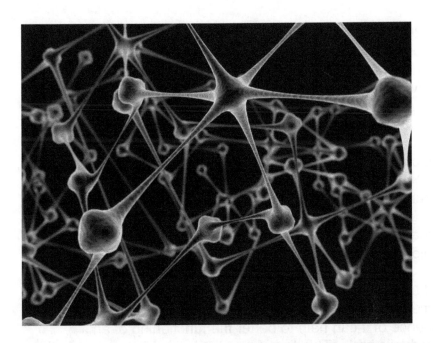

Gyrification is a word used to describe the development of new folds within the brain's cerebral cortex, which occur as a result of growth. Research suggests that gyrification might allow an individual's brain to process information at greater speeds. Some scientific experts also believe that this phenomenon could explain why some people are more efficient at processes like making decisions, recalling memories or focusing on their surroundings.

As recently as 2012, a scientific study identified greater gyrification rates in individuals who practice meditation. Another interesting brain change that is beginning to be linked to meditation is an increase in the thickness of the outer portion or cerebral cortex. This alteration can make an individual less sensitive to pain.

In a 2009 study from Aarhus University, Denmark, neuroscientists carefully compared the MRIs of individuals, who did not meditate, with the MRIs of individuals who often did. After such examination, they boldly declared, *"Long-term meditation is associated with increased grey matter density in the brain stem."*

This change in structure is believed to promote many benefits to those who meditate including superior cognitive abilities, immune responses, and emotional reactions. All this is attributed to the increase in grey matter density and its effects on the respiratory and heart rates, which in turn, yield greater cardiorespiratory control.

As it turns out, this gray matter plays a very important role in the central nervous system. Therefore, the increased presence of it can help to better the functioning of an individual's brain. This transformation can also be seen in the larger hippocampus and frontal lobes of individuals who meditate. The result is an increased ability to focus on daily tasks, a more optimistic outlook, and better mood control.

Another difference discovered requires a closer look at that grey matter over time. Meditation seems to reduce the effects of aging on certain brain tissue. This, in turn, slows the cognitive decline, which typically occurs as an individual ages.

One of the most recent studies has revealed that people who meditate also exhibit a unique manifestation of brain metabolites. This difference means a significantly decreased occurrence of mood disorders such as depression or anxiety.

Functional Changes

In addition to the visible chemical and physical changes to the brain, meditation also transforms the way an individual's brain works.

Meditating decreases the activity of the default mode network or DMN. DMN refers to areas of the brain that are typically most active during rest or inactivity. When a brain visits this mode too often, the individual may begin to exhibit signs of ADHD, or anxiety disorders. Physically, you might also note a build-up of beta-amyloid plaques, the substance tightly linked to Alzheimer's disease.

Another functional change in the way the brain works involves Theta and Alpha waves. These waves help regulate the brain's states of alert and relaxed attention. They can be measured using an EEG, or recording of the brain's electrical activity. Both of these types of brain waves show increased activity in individuals who practice meditation.

Meditation, General Wellbeing, and Healing

Medical studies show that the benefits of meditation travel far beyond the boundaries of the human brain.

Its practice correlates with numerous health benefits to the body. One of the biggest and most helpful factors is the reduction of stress, which of course is linked to the relaxing nature of meditation. It also may help to reverse the effects of heart disease, the leading cause of death in the United States. Meditation can also reduce the sensation of pain while strengthening the immune system, allowing a more effective battle against disease.

In 2012, a medical journal; 'Stroke' published an article featuring a study conducted on 60 African Americans who had been diagnosed with atherosclerosis. African Americans have been shown to be at nearly two times the risk of dying from cardiovascular disease in comparison to white individuals.

Atherosclerosis, or hardening of the arteries, is the number one cause of heart attacks. A group of the participants dedicated between six and nine months to a daily meditation practice. Those who meditated demonstrated a clear decrease in atherosclerosis present in the walls of their arteries. The individuals who abstained from meditation demonstrated an increase of atherosclerosis. When the numbers were crunched, meditating decreased the participants' heart attack risk by eleven percent in under a year. Meditation clearly reduces the experience of stress, slows respiration, calms the heart rate and reduces blood pressure levels.

A separate study included 90 cancer patients. A random grouping of the participants were instructed how to practice mindful meditation. Seven weeks later, those who meditated reported better mental health including less depression, anxiety, and confusion. They also reported a significantly lower rate of gastrointestinal or heart-related complaints.

So how does meditation create such positive changes?

We have previously discussed the changes that occur inside the brain. One of the additional changes is a decrease in the stress hormone Cortisol. This alteration allows individuals a chance to react to stressors and stressful situations in a more efficient manner.

In a 2012 study, individuals who had practiced meditation for eight weeks performed significantly better on a multitasking stress test than those who had not meditated. Researchers believe this may be explained through a reduced presence of Cortisol.

Practicing meditation prior to a potentially stressful event can decrease the level of stress experienced during that encounter or event. It can also improve the quality of the sleep you get each night.

We all know sleep is a vital component in assuming good mental and physical health.

According to a study conducted by the University of Utah, individuals who meditate report greater emotional control during the day. The researchers attributed the participant's improved mental functions during the day to less activity, and greater rest acquired during a good night's sleep.

Developing Empathy

In addition to reducing stress levels, meditation changes and improves the ways in which individuals interact with one another. Therapists have reported that their clients argue and bicker less with their loved ones once they begin to practice meditation. They appear less angry, more reflective, loving, and compassionate.

In short, meditation raises an individual's level of empathy for others. One form of meditation, which is particularly effective at developing this skill, is called loving-kindness-compassion meditation. While grounded in the shaky world of emotion, researchers have spent countless hours verifying this transformation, rooting its validity through the world of science.

One particular study compared the MRIs of individuals who casually practiced meditation with those of a more expert level, namely Buddhist monks with over 10,000 hours of meditation experience. As emotional stimuli affected these individuals, the empathy region of the brain would light up with increased activity. The monks consistently showed a more exaggerated response to meditation than that demonstrated by the newcomers. This led scientists to confirm that meditation has the ability to increase an individual's ability to empathize with others.

Experts trace this change to meditation's insistence on removes your perspective from the ego. When an individual develops a greater sense of self through meditation, the ego begins to dissipate. As meditation heightens your awareness, they remember that we are all connected. This realization adds a more accurate perspective on life's interactions.

Accessing New Ideas

Open-monitoring meditation, or OM, is an effective tool for generating ideas. Creative individuals such as writers, artists, or inventors often utilize it.

In stark contrast to focused attention meditation practices, OM participants tune in their minds without reacting or influencing the content. Physiological science has demonstrated that the mindfulness acquired through meditation can open previous "blind spots" in an individual's thoughts and perceptions. This opens a completely new world of ideas, visions, and self-knowledge, which can translate as confidence and creativity.

Mind and body work together. Meditation improves the way the brain works. Individuals who meditate are sharper and more mindful. These concepts are behind a popular study published in *'Emotion';* a psychology journal stating that during meditation, an individual focuses the mind on breathing or physical sensations, not allowing it to wander too far off course or delve too deeply into tangents. This activity improves an individual's memory skills, problem-solving abilities, and complex thought processes.

Changing the Way You Perceive the World

The power of meditation beholds both long and short-term benefits in relation to the way an individual perceives their environment and their peers.

During 1984, a study (Brown et al), was performed on the maximum threshold for the perception of a stimulus in the form of light. The participants were a mix of individuals, some who practiced meditation and others who did not. At the end of the study, it was confirmed that those who meditate have a lower threshold for detecting a short light stimulus.

The researchers' explanation for this phenomenon theorizes that "[the higher rate of detection of single light flashes] involves quieting some of the higher mental processes which normally obstruct the perception of subtle events". Put another way, the process of meditation transforms, either permanently or temporarily, the top to bottom manner in which the mind processes subtle information, which cues the power of perception.

A separate study (Tloczynski *et al.,* 2000), observed perception in the context of visual illusions including one termed the Poggendorff Illusion. The Poggendorff illusion utilizes a common misperception created by the removal of one portion of a pair of transverse lines. When the perceptions of meditation beginners, meditation experts, and individuals who did not practice meditation at all were compared, it was shown that the experts, also labeled Zen-masters, had a significant advantage demonstrated in a reduction of the volume of errors recorded.

In closing the researcher states;

> "A person who meditates consequently perceives objects more as directly experienced stimuli and less as concepts... With the removal or minimization of cognitive stimuli and generally increasing awareness, meditation can, therefore, influence both the quality (accuracy) and quantity (detection) of perception."

Along the road to positive thoughts and optimism is a sunny spot known as happiness. People who meditate are also generally happier than those who do not. One scientific study, which relates to this fact, was conducted on a group of individuals suffering from multiple sclerosis. Although an exclusive group, it can be said that those suffering from such a debilitating disease might be expected to be more depressed than the general population.

The participants discussed in *'Neurology'* journal, presented mild to moderate cases of Multiple Sclerosis. Over the course of eight weeks, these individuals were engaged in the instruction of mindful meditation. When the classes were completed, the researchers observed that the rate of depression had decreased among the recipients by at least thirty percent. They also reported decreased symptoms of fatigue.

Separate studies conducted in Wisconsin discovered that individuals that regularly participated in meditation demonstrated greater electrical activity in the left prefrontal cortex of the brain. The particular area is typically associated with a positive disposition.

Duration

One useful skill, which is improved through meditation, is that of focused attention. A 2010 study took a closer look at the attention spans of individuals as they practiced five hours of daily meditation for a duration of three months. After three months of rigorous meditation, they retook concentrations tests, at which they showed a significant increase in the ability to maintain voluntary attention.

This is not surprising when you consider the nature of meditation. The practice can require long periods of concentration. It makes sense then, that practicing this skill would improve an individual's ability to focus on other tasks. Meditation is not a secular task; it can affect all aspects of an individual's life.

It may be encouraging to note that you need not practice five hours of daily meditation to reap the benefits. Lucky are those who have such an ample amount of time to devote to the task. Many studies indicate that a mere 2 to 20 minutes a day is sufficient to see significant results in the way of stress reduction, concentration, and emotional stability.

Only a little meditating is necessary to discover its benefits. One study indicates that these positive transformations begin to take place immediately. Great progress has been seen over the course of as few as ten days. These changes include increased mindfulness and thoughtfulness, decreased depressive tendencies, greater memory skills, and improved concentration.

That said, the longer an individual continues to meditate, the more profound the benefits appear to become. A lifetime commitment to simple, daily meditation is perhaps the best way to improve the health of your body and mind and to minimize the hazards of aging.

What do I need to start Meditating (Clue: Not much!)

One of the beauties of meditation is that at its core you require nothing other than your own body to practice it.

While other sports and activities demand special equipment and training you can relax in the knowledge you already have everything you need, and best of all you carry it around with you 24 hours a day!

That's not to say there aren't some physical and mental aids that will help; just that usually they aren't needed. If someone is obsessed with getting all the proper kit before starting it is often a sign that they either aren't mentally prepared or that they are postponing beginning for some reason.

(See 'The 2 Minute Secret' section for more on this)

Recommended Aids to Meditation:

1. **Motivation:** The will to act is the foundation of Meditation practice. This is where it all begins and hopefully, some of the content in this guide can help with that.

2. **Space:** A little room is also a big help. You don't need a remote mountain-top monastery, just enough space for you to be comfortable in your chosen position.

3. **Peace and Quiet:** While you may eventually become skilled enough to fully focus even in noisy environments, as you start out a quiet place will be a big help.

4. **Time** (Only 2 Minutes to start with).

5. **Focus Object:** This depends on the type of meditation you are aiming for but a simple candle can be an excellent focal point.

6. **Music/Guidance:** Again depending on your chosen style you might find soft ambient music beneficial. Or, if you are following a set routine, a guided voice recording can also be a big help.

7. **Support:** A cushion or 'Zafu' may also help to support your position…

EXERCISE THREE:

Write down a list of all the things you think you need to get started in meditation. Done? Good, now eliminate all but three of those things, focusing purely on the most important ones. Be brutally honest and zero in on the ones you require, not the ones you want.

You now have a list of the things you *really* need.

Meditation Cushions (and do you need one?)

Meditation Cushions

While seeking your ideal meditation position, it might also be helpful to learn about meditation cushions. There are a number of cushions and props to help support these positions and assist the goal of proper alignment. While not required, a good cushion can be a valuable ally in discovering a comfortable position, which makes establishing a routine easier.

These cushions come in a multitude of shapes, sizes, and colors. While it would be difficult to discuss all of the options available, below you will find a brief discussion of the three most common varieties. These include the zafu, rectangular, and crescent cushions.

Meditation cushions are typically filled with either buckwheat or kapok. Kapok is a fluffy material similar to cotton, while buckwheat grains are small and firm. Kapok is softer while the buckwheat hulls maintain their shape and contour to the shape of your body. Choosing between the two is a strictly personal decision. If possible try to feel each type before purchasing.

Your own size, shape, height, and level of flexibility will determine the best cushion height, fabric, and filling. While it can be fun and exciting to choose meditation accessories in bright colors and bold patterns, keep your goals in mind. You might be better served to choose a calm palate to help center the mind and avoid unnecessary distraction.

Zafu Cushion

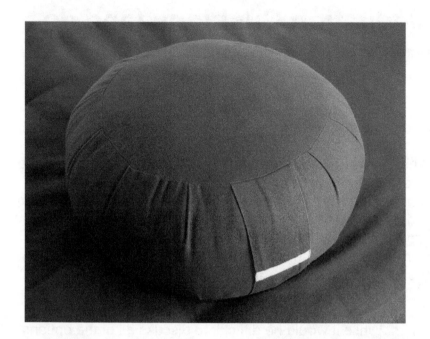

A traditional Zafu cushion has a round shape with pleats all along the sides. It can be used to raise your hips, allowing the legs to be more comfortable, and creating a more natural alignment of the spine.

While it was originally designed as a companion for the Burmese position, it can also be used for the seiza positioning (kneeling). To use this sort of cushion sit on the edge, allowing your thighs to slightly slope downward,

The zafu is best for individuals of average height, and a reasonable degree of flexibility.

Rectangular Cushion

This rectangle shaped cushion is simple in form. It is not as high as a zafu, though it is designed for easy stacking. The rectangular cushion is ideal for those of average to short stature and those with ample flexibility. Individuals who are especially tall or possess only limited flexibility might use a rectangular cushion paired with a zafu to create a more comfortable height

Crescent Cushion

The crescent cushion is a special kind of zafu cushion. Its name is derived from the shape, which is reminiscent of a crescent moon. This cushion is best designed for the cross-legged or Burmese positions. It features ample sitting room and elevates the legs, which can help maintain proper circulation. The height of most crescent style cushions can be adjusted by taking away or adding additional filling through an opening at the rear of the cushion.

The crescent cushion can be the ideal meditation cushion for anyone since it can be customized by each user. It is a particularly good choice for those of higher stature or larger build.

Cushions aren't compulsory by any means, and many people find they are flexible enough or comfortable without one but if you find it difficult to achieve a good posture or a relaxed position they can offer some support. Literally.

Meditation For Your Everyday

It is possible to increase your ability to concentrate and reduce stress without learning meditation terminology such as "chakra". Yoga wear, incense, and philosophical discussion are not required either. You also will not need to sign up for a mountain retreat, (although they really can be an amazing experience). The only thing you will need to meditate is the ability to breathe. Simple as that.

A daily practice is recommended for the absolute best way to see the benefits of meditation. As previously mentioned regularity is the key to success.

The techniques in this guide may seem simple, perhaps overly so, but this is part of the point; effective and powerful meditation can be simple and easy to perform. In fact, by overcomplicating the process you are reducing the chances of maintaining any daily routine.

By practicing daily meditation you will soon discover just how far your mind is capable of wandering from the task at hand. Our world is full of distractions not the least of which being internet surfing and over-booked schedules. Being able to focus can become an invaluable tool. Meditation is a way to exercise your mind, increasing its functionality, lowering stress, and even increasing the ability to forgive.

Daily meditation is the perfect opportunity to slow down for a moment, to pay attention to your own mind, and to focus on your breath, and although meditation primarily began as a religious practice within the Hindu and Buddhist faiths, today's version isn't necessarily connected to any form of religion at all.

In essence, mindful meditation plays a role in many faiths; however, faith does not necessarily play a part in the art of meditation. By introducing a daily practice you can shape it any way you wish.

Meditation Positions: Choosing the Right One for You

(Sitting, Standing, Or Lying?)

Being an immensely personal practice, meditation can take many forms. The postures assumed by its practitioners are every bit as varied as the thoughts within their minds. It is most often done in a seated position, though individuals can meditate while walking, or during simple, repetitive tasks.

While there is no restriction on the seating arrangement you choose, there are five common positions that are often taken up. It may be useful to become acquainted with these positions and try each one yourself.

Above all, it is always more important to choose an arrangement which is most comfortable to you. As always, we are trying to reduce the obstacles to relaxation.

Discomfort will only provide a distraction from your practice, hindering your ability to devote the full attention which meditation requires. Remember that meditation requires a state of mindful relaxation. What is best for one is not necessarily right for another, and that is perfectly fine. Choose your own meditation tools.

In addition to comfort, there are a few important factors to consider when choosing a meditation position. The best pose will provide stability, and support for your frame. It will also provide proper alignment of four vital points of your body. These include the neck, head, spine, and shoulders. These factors will aid your endurance in maintaining the chosen position for any extended length of time.

The common meditation positions include:

1. Burmese

2. Chair sitting

3. Full-Lotus

4. Half-Lotus

5. Seiza (Kneeling)

Burmese

This is perhaps the easiest meditation position and the most commonly seen. It is characterized by crossed legs and feet, which rest flat against the ground. Ideally, your knees should also lie against the ground, if the participant possesses enough flexibility. Stretching can aid this position by helping the legs descend until the knees meet the floor.

Still, this should be done gradually and may take both time and practice to master. One way to encourage this is to utilize a Zafu cushion (see Cushions section), sitting at the front portion, and balancing your bodyweight ever so slightly forward. Picture the crown of your head pressing up towards the sky, creating a stretch, which moves through your body, straightening the spine. Finally, allow your body and breath to relax, slackening the tautness of your muscles.

A benefit of choosing this position is that it requires little effort to remain upright once seated.

Chair Sitting

The chair sitting posture seems simplistic in nature, and to some degree, it is.

Still, it may take some finesse to develop good form. First, choose a chair with a solid, supportive back. Then sit up tall and ever so slightly tilt forward, avoiding the innate tendency to fold against the back of the chair. The feet should be spread to shoulder width apart while resting flat against the ground.

Your knees should assume as near a 90-degree angle as possible. A cushion might be used to elevate the feet to create more stability or help create that 90-degree angle. Individuals with troublesome backs might benefit from a second cushion placed near the lower region of their back.

Note that the spine is kept straight, freeing the movements of the diaphragm through each breath. The lower back is gently bent, following its natural curve. Both thighs travel from the pelvis region towards the knees in a very slight slope so to tilt the pelvis to the front. This positioning provides support for the lower back and is comfortable for most individuals. The vertical alignment created by this pose helps promote the free flow of energy throughout the body.

Note that while sitting in a chair is a valid option, it is not considered an ideal or traditional position in many systems. There is also the risk of being dependent on the availability of a proper chair in order to reach a meditative state.

Full Lotus (or 'Lotus Position')

The Lotus Position finds its origins in ancient India's Hindu Yoga practices. From there it was borrowed by Buddhists, who began utilizing the form for meditation. The position is meant to resemble the Lotus, a beautiful water lily native to Asia and northern Australia.

In full lotus, each foot is placed against the thigh of the opposite leg. The pose supports proper breathing practices. The full lotus position is also characterized by symmetry, efficiency, and stability. These aspects make sitting cross-legged, on the ground, a wise option.

Not everyone will feel comfortable in the full lotus position at first; in fact, it can be a bit challenging to those with limited flexibility. It may be wise for those individuals to attempt the Half Lotus position and work up to the full position.

One must be careful not to strain the hips or lower back while utilizing this position. Take care not to stretch beyond your abilities, and do not force your body to hold the pose past the point of comfort.

Half Lotus

In the Half Lotus position, one foot rests upon the opposite thigh beneath which the alternate leg is carefully tucked. Unlike the full lotus position, the half lotus lacks perfect symmetry. It may be necessary to make adjustments in the way the upper body is balanced in order to maintain a straight alignment of the spine.

If you choose to practice in the half lotus, be sure to alternate the leg which is brought up as opposed to being folded beneath. Once the body is adjusted, this position becomes comfortable and offers good support as well as proper circulation. It only requires a moderate degree of flexibility. Still, some individuals might find this position uncomfortable, and even impossible to maintain for long stretches of time.

Seiza (Kneeling)

The Seiza position is ideal for people who lack flexibility, particularly in the hip region. With origins in the Far East, it is a position commonly also seen in traditional Japanese Martial Arts such as Karate, Aikido and Iaido

It is also one of the easiest positions to get into or release. Here the individual assumes a kneeling position, with the knees carefully placed shoulder-width apart. Your buttocks remain solidly supported by the heels, which cradle it at either side.

The practitioner might choose to utilize a low, modified bench, or sitting cushion to make the position more relaxed and therefore comfortable. A pillow might also help to relieve the weight of your body from the ankles. As in the other positions, the spine is kept straight and the lower back in a natural curve creating proper vertical alignment. Many individuals find the Seiza position to be spiritually grounding. On the flipside, this posture remains uncomfortable for some people and it can be difficult to hold for extended lengths of time.

Lying Down

Since relaxation plays such a vital role in the meditation process, it might then seem to make sense that lying down would be a good position to work in. While it can be an option for some individuals, meditating while lying down can be a little tricky and is generally not recommended unless for the "Body Scan" method.

The biggest trouble is that you may find yourself fighting, and possibly giving in to the temptation to fall asleep. While both are highly beneficial, sleeping and meditation do not make good partners. You need to be conscious in order to meditate. If you choose to lie down while meditating, do so with caution. Be sure that you begin your meditation session well rested to reduce the risk of drifting off into dreamland.

Top Tip No. 1 - The Power of Being in the Present

There are hundreds of forms of meditation and many different physical positions you can use. A number of the most effective ones are included in this book but perhaps the single most powerful driving concept behind almost every form of meditation is 'being in the present'.

We spend so much of our life planning, plotting and working out where and who we want to be. It's only natural after all to have dreams and desires. But continually focusing on the future is an extremely fast way to get stressed.

The future isn't here. We can't directly affect it right now so why spend all of our time thinking about it?

The same is true of the past. How many times have you regretted something, caught yourself remembering former loves or times you wish you could have changed?

So much of our time is spent looking forward and back at the infinite possibilities of what might be that we hardly ever focus on what is.

A core concept of almost every form of meditation is to switch off these thoughts of past and future and just be.

Don't worry about what was, or what could be. There is just the here and now. Fully focus on the sensations and feelings of the moment you are in, and only that moment.

Anytime you feel stressed or wish to calm your thoughts, begin by thinking *"how do I feel right now?"*

Top Tip No.2 - Don't Judge

The second most important recurring theme within mindfulness is the idea of accepting what is happening in the moment without passing judgment.

We live in an incredibly complex world where a thousand things demand our attention at once. The analytical part of your brain, the part that solves problems is constantly trying to work out what is going on around you and how you can succeed in negotiating this crazy life.

But because the modern life is more demanding than ever, we overwhelm our minds with analytical, calculating thoughts. Trying to figure things out even when we don't need to.

One of the fantastic concepts behind meditation is again to switch off this judgemental part of your mind. Effectively giving your brain some downtime.

Think about how good you feel when resting after intense exercise. The same is true of your mind.

Switching off and giving your brain some well-earned recuperation is as simple as:

1. **Not thinking of the future or the past. Just being here and now.**
2. **Accepting how you feel and not judging it in any way.**

Combining these concepts is a simple and incredibly healing process, even for a short time such as two minutes. Simply sit quietly, be in the present and feel how you feel.

You don't need to do anything and you don't need to think anything. This is the beauty of mindfulness.

Your Two Minute Meditation Schedule

Begin now to think about your own meditation practice and how you will set up a simple schedule that you will easily keep.

Look at each day and make a note of the times you are A. Most stressed and B. Most calm.

Meditation and relaxation exercises during periods of extreme stress can be very beneficial, but as a beginner, it is usually too much to attempt to calm the mind under these circumstances until you have some experience.

Similarly meditating during periods of deep calm run the risk of triggering drowsiness and sleep.

Sleep is a great thing, but it is not meditation!

To begin with, try to find a point in the day when you are somewhere in between stressed and relaxed. A kind of middle ground.

This doesn't have to be fixed forever, the aim is simply to give you the best possible chance of establishing and sticking to a routine as you start out.

Once you have practiced 2 Minutes a day for 2 weeks, at your original chosen time, you can now think about moving the period of the day in which you do it.

You will quickly find you get better at the process and see the relaxation response kicking in.

Perhaps the biggest benefit of meditation is the pleasure of a few minutes spent sitting, in a relaxing center of calm. With today's busy lifestyles those few minutes can feel absolutely priceless. Keep in mind that the goal isn't necessarily to become professional, but to let a few minutes of meditation into your life every day.

The following steps may seem simple because we have, in our busy lives, become accustomed to undertaking extremely complicated and difficult processes to achieve results. However, Two Minute Meditation strips away all this in favor of a minimalistic approach and herein lies its strength.

If we can remove the confusion and noise of daily life and spend just a few minutes in a space of calm we return the body to a more natural, relaxed and positive state.

EXERCISE FOUR:

Make a note of which times of the day you are running around like a crazy person, and which times you are most at peace. Find a point where you have your own time and space and where you are neither fully stressed or fully relaxed.

For many this will be after the initial morning dash to work or school but before they relax for the evening. A point around lunchtime or mid-morning can work well.

This will be your ideal starting point.

The Steps to Take:

1. Commit: Make a promise to yourself to make meditation a daily habit. Pledge to meditate for at least two minutes a day. You can always practice for longer if you wish but think of two minutes as your bare minimum.

2. Schedule: Ensure that you will stick to your commitment by planning meditation into your day. You do not necessarily need to choose an exact start time. Instead, write down your intention to meditate every morning when waking up, or during your daily lunch break.

3. Trigger: A trigger is an action which you already perform that can serve as a reminder that it is time to meditate. Pick something simple such as brushing your teeth, pouring a cup of coffee, eating lunch, or returning home after work.

4. Location: Find a quiet spot where you will not be distracted. If you have children or roommates, it would be wise to plan for a morning meditation practice before anyone else will be awake. Other pleasant meditation locations include your backyard, the park, or on a beach.

5. Get Comfortable: It is not so important what you wear or how you sit, as it is for you to be comfortable during meditation. You might decide to sit in a chair, on the floor with a pillow, cross-legged, on a Zafu, a yoga mat, or leaning against the wall.

6. Begin: Find your trigger, location, get comfortable and dive into your first two-minute meditation. In your comfortable position simply start by being still for a couple of minutes (See 'How to Begin earlier in this guide). If you can go longer then feel free to continue. Most individuals will find that they can easily meditate for fifteen to twenty minutes once they begin. However, it is more important to practice every day than to keep going for an extended period of time. Try growing your meditations with baby steps. When you are comfortable with two-minutes, try five or seven, when seven becomes easy move up to ten minutes.

7. Focus: Meditation required focus. Now pay attention to your breath as you inhale through your nose, filling your lungs and belly before slowly exhaling through your mouth. Try to sit up straight, with your eyes open towards the ground, with a very gentle focus. If this is too distracting, then go ahead and close your eyes. To keep your mind focused you may opt to count each breath. (After a month of continued practice you can officially declare that you have successfully made meditation a daily habit!)

8. Expand: Once meditation has become a regular part of your day, consider ways that you can grow your practice. Since you have now developed an ability to remain mindful you will be able to apply this skill in many ways.

- If you find yourself in a stressful situation, try to stop and take a moment to become aware of your breath. This will help return your mind to the here and now.

- Try a walking meditation. Rather than let your mind wander, focus on your breath, the sensations within your body, and the world that surrounds you.

- Become more mindful of what you eat. Instead of hurrying to finish a meal, focus on your food. Pay close attention to colors, flavors, and sensations as you eat.

- Sip a mug of warm tea. Become mindful of each subtle movement as you first prepare your tea. Smell the aroma. Taste your tea. Remember to breathe and savor each moment.

- Turn menial household chores into an escape. Try applying mindfulness as you wash the dishes, fold laundry, or sweep the floor. Pay attention to each movement and the results of your efforts.

There is no limit to the ways in which you can use mindful meditation to improve your quality of life. Try to think of additional ways you can introduce more moments of mindfulness to your day. A dedicated meditation can affect your attitude throughout the day, your interactions with others, and your efficiency at work. Begin your own meditation practice today. Why not take a few minutes right now to melt away stress and become more present in this very moment.

Summary:

1. **Commit:** Promise yourself to develop a Meditation habit
2. **Schedule:** Roughly plan when you will Meditate
3. **Trigger:** Establish a time or activity that will remind you to begin
4. **Location:** Find a quiet place where you will not be

disturbed
5. **Get Comfortable:** Find a comfy position, and try to remain still
6. **Begin:** With everything in place it's time to start
7. **Focus:** Start by focusing on your breath (and counting if this helps)
8. **Expand:** With the basics in place explore doing more with Meditation

Easy Relaxation

When you look at the physiology of the human body, the term relaxation occurs when balance is restored to the nervous system. The opposite of relaxation is stress.

In order to live, an individual will encounter stress which is broken down into two categories, *eustress,* and *distress.* Eustress is the positive kind which motivates an individual and focuses their energy towards short-term goals. Eustress encourages creativity, learning and improved survival techniques. Distress is the harmful kind which can grow over time, disrupting the body's equilibrium. Distress causes anxiety, decreases an individual's performance and endangers the nervous system's equilibrium.

For most individuals today, life seems packed with a tremendous amount of stress. Relaxations techniques involving meditation can be used to bring the nervous system back towards equilibrium, by producing what is called the *relaxation response.* The relaxation response is characterized by a profound calmness.

When your body comes under stress, it reacts by besieging your nervous system with chemicals which ready the body for a *fight or flight response.* In an emergency, the fight or flight response can your life. However, it also requires a lot of energy to maintain. When the stressor does not go away, such as in the case of everyday stressors, your body becomes exhausted. The relaxation response is needed to calm this heightened readiness and return both body and mind to a balanced state.

Generating the Relaxation Response

The most effective relaxation technique may vary from one individual to the next. It is worth stating that when we use the term relaxation in this context we are not talking about lying on the couch, watching television, or sleeping. This form of relaxation is a state in where the mind is active yet calm and focused which encourages physical relaxation.

Most relaxation techniques are not complicated or difficult to learn. Though, it may take time and practice to cultivate these skills. It is recommended that you begin by taking five or ten minutes each day to practice your relaxation techniques. Certainly thirty minutes to an hour will provide even more benefits eventually. Such an investment may seem difficult at first, but most individuals can easily incorporate relaxation techniques into their daily schedule. Consider practicing at your desk during lunch, on the bus on the way to work, or in the evening before setting into bed.

How to Relax the Right Way for You

No relaxation technique will work for everyone. It may take a little experimentation to discover the best method for you. Some variables to consider are your goals, personal preferences, fitness level, the manner in which you tend to react to stress, and which kinds of stressors trigger the most intense responses.

Choose the technique which sounds the most pleasant, fits into your daily life, and is effective at focusing your mind past routine thoughts to create the relaxation response. You may find that combining two techniques together or fluctuating between techniques yields the greatest success. If the first technique does not work for you, then simply try another.

Things to Consider

1. How do you respond to stressors?

Stress Style	Indicators	Recommended Techniques
Frozen	Individual is immobilized by fear, or shock. The body slows while internal processes speed up.	Choose a stimulating technique which also holds a sense of security. Power yoga or mindful walking are good options.
Over Excited	Individual becomes angry and/or agitated.	Choose a calming and quieting technique such as meditation, deep breathing work, or imagery.
Under Excited	Individual withdraws, becomes depressed, and/or spacey.	Choose a stimulating technique like rhythmic exercise to revitalize the nervous system.

2. Are you social or introverted?

When you feel stressed are you more likely to seek out solitude or friends? Individuals who prefer alone time should focus on private relaxation techniques like progressive muscle relaxation or deep breathing meditation. These kinds of tasks will provide an opportunity to bring your mind to a quiet place and reenergize your body.

Individuals who prefer social situations should seek relaxation techniques which are available in a classroom setting. These kinds of techniques will present the stimulation and support you need. Practicing relaxation techniques with other people can also provide motivation to continue.

How to Relax Anywhere (Switching off Stress and Noise)

I remember several years ago I found myself in arguably one of the most stressful places on earth; Times Square - New York City. If you've never been I encourage it just for the assault on the senses.

Everything is loud, flashing and screaming for your attention. As if this wasn't enough I was also stuck in traffic and desperately lost. (I was supposed to be leaving the city and had instead ended up right in the middle!).

It was stressful, panic-inducing and I quickly found I felt less and less in control as my thoughts spiraled around.

Then I recalled some of my experiences in China and the Far East regarding Meditation and Qi Gong, in particular, some of the approaches to quieting the mind regardless of your surroundings.

I was shocked by just how quickly a little self-awareness was able to lower my stress and induce a sense of focused calm even though I was far from an expert at this.

There are several approaches to finding your own sweet spot amid the torrent of distractions around you. Next time you are in a busy Train station, Office, or surrounded by noise consider the following;

1. Accept It

The first step is to accept what is happening around you. Noise, motion, whatever. Don't try to change it, just be aware of it fully with all of your conscience and accept it is there.

Once you are aware of it, don't dwell on it. Don't let it irritate you or concern you. It's there and you have accepted that.

2. What You Can Control

In a stressful situation often the only thing you can control is yourself; your body and mind.

Try to bring the body to stillness, reduce any fidgeting and movement and find a comfortable position. (This doesn't have to be a traditional meditation position)

Gently draw your thoughts into a focus point. The easiest method is usually to focus on your breathing, being aware of each inhalation and exhalation.

3. Find the Gaps

Once you have accepted the surroundings and controlled your own body, next try to find the 'gaps' or the 'space' in the noise around you. Expand your thoughts and try to become aware of the silence in which the noise sits or the stillness in which the movement exists.

Imagine the chair you sit on now. It also exists within a certain space. An object in a room dwells in its own space too.

For every sound there is also silence surrounding it; the 'space' in which it lives.

For every movement, there is similarly stillness.

Each cannot exist without the other so try to sense it and draw calm from this.

These aren't always easy notions to master and this technique can be even harder if you have not first accepted the surroundings and controlled your body but it can be an incredibly powerful method to give you an amazing 'calm at the center of the storm' sensation amid the hustle and bustle around you.

"Meditation is the dissolution of thoughts in Eternal awareness or pure consciousness without objectification, knowing without thinking, merging finitude in infinity."

-Voltaire

The Relaxation and Meditation Techniques

The following are examples of a number of Meditation and Mindfulness techniques that may work for you. As we have already established, meditation is a deeply personal experience and so one technique here that works for you may not work for others.

Try a selection of them out and see which one fits you best.

Similarly, try not to expect too much when you begin. Simply act and feel, rather than judge.

Technique One: Deep Breathing Meditation

Deep breathing meditation focuses on cleansing breaths. Practicing deep breathing is an uncomplicated and effective technique for achieving relaxation. This skill is simple to teach and can be performed in nearly any location to promptly reduce your stress levels.

Due to its efficacy, you will see deep breathing in many other relaxation practices. It can be paired with other relaxation essentials like music or aromatherapy, but all you really need is a few moments and some space to get comfortable.

To begin you will need to practice breathing deeply from your abdomen. Take in as much air as you can. By breathing from your abdomen and not the upper chest, you will receive more oxygen. More oxygen inhaled means your body becomes less tense. You won't feel short of breath and your anxiety level will decrease.

Below is a short deep breathing meditation. In the case that you have trouble breathing from your abdomen while in a seated position, try the meditation reclined on the floor. Another suggestion is to place a small book upon the stomach. Try to take deep breaths with enough strength to raise and lower the book as you inhale and exhale respectively.

1. Begin seated in a comfortable position and with a straightened back. Place one of your hands over your chest and the second hand over your stomach.

2. Inhale through your nose and notice how the hand over your stomach begins to rise. Also, note that the hand over your chest stays fairly still.

3. Release the breath through your mouth. Exhale as much air as possible while contracting your abs. Notice the hand over your stomach falling in while the hand over your chest continues to stay fairly still.

4. Repeat the process, inhaling through the nose, exhaling through the mouth. See if you can breathe in deep enough to cause the lower abdomen to move as well. Leisurely count through each exhalation.

EXERCISE FIVE

Find a quiet place and take a seat. Straighten your back, open your chest and try the Deep Breathing Meditation process listed, for just two minutes.

Initially, don't worry about taking the process further or reaching some higher state of consciousness. Just be present and breathe.

Technique Two: Progressive muscle relaxation

This relaxation technique relies on a two-step process. You will first tense and then relax each muscle group. Practicing progressive muscle relaxation is a way to remind yourself how tension feels in opposition to how complete relaxation feels.

The renewed awareness within your body will help you identify moments when you beginning to take on the tension in reaction to stress. Eventually, you will be able to practice this technique at the first hints of stress, relaxing your body, and also your mind. To increase the effectiveness of progressive muscle relaxation you can try pairing it with the deep breathing technique described in the last section.

It is recommended that anyone with a medical history of back problems, muscle spasms, or serious injuries receive the approval of their physician before trying progressive muscle relaxation. Ailments such as these can become aggravated through tensing muscles.

Before starting, get comfortable by loosening your clothing and removing your shoes. Take some time to get centered and relax by bringing your attention to your breath as you inhale and exhale slowly. When you are ready, begin at your feet and gradually work your way up through the muscle groups until you reach your face.

1. Gradually squeeze to tense the muscles within your right foot as tight as possible. Count to ten as you hold the squeeze. (Left-handed individuals may find it more comfortable to begin on the left side.)

2. Release the tension in your right foot. Pay attention to the tension as it leaves relaxation behind. Notice your foot become loose and limp.

3. Remain in that relaxed state for a few moments as you slowly inhale and exhale.

4. Now tense your left foot. Holding, releasing and relaxing as you did with the right.

5. Continue on through the muscle groups, tensing and relaxing each one. It may take practice before you are able to focus enough to contract only the intended muscles. The chart below will provide a rough guide as you continue on through your body.

- Right Foot (Or left if left handed)
- Left Foot (or Alternate)
- Right Calf Region
- Left Calf Region
- Right Thigh Region
- Left Thigh Region
- Hips & Buttocks Area
- Stomach and Abdominal Area
- Chest
- Back

- Right Arm & Hand (and fingers)
- Left Arm & Hand (and Fingers)
- Shoulders & Neck Region
- Face

EXERCISE SIX

It's incredibly easy for us to hold tension in our bodies without realizing it. For this exercise, we will find that tension and gently release it.

When you are next at home, find a space where you can lie down and relax—but not too much—we don't want to fall asleep.

Then, begin the *Progressive Muscle Relaxation* Technique and work down your own body, using the method described. Find, recognize and release tension along the way.

Technique Three: Body Scan Meditation

This relaxation technique is much like progressive muscle relaxation. The big difference is that you simply becomes aware of your body while focusing on sensations within each area instead of tensing or relaxing muscles.

1. Begin resting on your back with your arms relaxed and at your sides. Be sure not to cross your legs. Keep your eyes open or closed depending on whichever is most comfortable for you.

2. Bring your attention to your breath. Notice your stomach rise and fall with each inhalation and exhalation. Spend two minutes breathing deeply, allowing your body and mind to relax.

3. Now shift your focus to the toes on your right foot. Become aware of any sensations originating there, while continuing to notice your breath. Picture each inhalation as the air moves towards your toes. Stay focused in this region for a minute or two.

4. Bring your attention down to the sole of your foot. Become aware of any sensations originating there, picture the air from each breath flowing from this region. Stay focused here for a minute or two before shifting to your ankle of the same foot.

5. Continue this routine as you travel from the ankle to the calf, knee, thigh, and hip before moving on to your left leg.

6. Once you have completed both legs, travel up your torso to the lower back and abdominal regions, the upper back and chest, and then your shoulders. Spend extra time in any area that is bringing particular discomfort or pain.

7. Next, you will focus on your fingers of the right hand. Then move to your wrist, onto the forearm area and elbow, to the upper arm, and shoulder before repeating the corresponding regions on your left arm.

8. Focus on your neck, and then your throat before moving to your face. Pay attention to your jaw region and chin, lips and mouth, tongue area, nose, the cheeks, around the eyes, forehead muscles, temples, and then the whole scalp. Spend a minute at the back and crown of your head.

9. As you near the top of your head, exhale and reach up above your body. Picture yourself hovering up above your own body.

10. Spend a few minutes in quiet relaxation. Lie still, taking note of the way your body is feeling.

11. Open your eyes, and stretch gently.

EXERCISE SEVEN

Starting in the same way as the previous exercise, find a space where you can fully stretch out and relax.

Then, take a couple of minutes to bring the attention to the bottom of your feet and work your way up the body using the Body Scan Technique described. Once again, find and release tension along the way.

Technique Four: Mindfulness

Mindfulness is an important skill. It is the ability to maintain awareness of the way you feel both inside and outside at any moment. Mindfulness keeps an individual grounded in the here and now. Contemplating the past, entertaining judgments or regrets, or fretting about tomorrow will tend to create a sensation of stress, often to an extent that becomes overwhelming. Mindfulness will assist you in staying calm and present in the moment. It also helps return the nervous system back into a state of balance.

This technique can be practiced through a wide range of activities like walking, eating, or exercising. Mindful meditations are a tried and true method of stress reduction. Here your attention will turn to the breath, a simple repeated phrase, or the flame of a candle. Meanwhile, alternative types of mindful meditation work by following and then releasing various thoughts or sensations as they come into awareness.

1. Find a quiet area where you can have some privacy. It can be within your home, office, garden, place of worship, or outside. Meditation can be practiced anywhere that you are able to relax free of distractions.

2. Make yourself comfortable. Try to remain seated either on the floor or in a chair, lying down may cause you to fall asleep. Straighten your spine. You may even want to try a lotus position.

3. Choose a focal point. This can be internal or external. Focus on a feeling, an image in your mind, an object, a candle's flame, a word or a phrase. You may choose to keep your eyes opened or closed depending on what is most comfortable.

4. Try to maintain an observant yet non-judgmental mindset. Allow your thoughts to move through your mind as you shift back to your focal point. Try not to waste energy worrying about whether you are doing this right. Remember, the goal is relaxation.

EXERCISE EIGHT

Mindfulness is one of the most powerful meditation exercises available, so if you try only one method, make it this one.

Start by sitting in a relaxed but upright position and breathe in and out slowly, then focus your mind and follow the *Mindfulness* process, being present and non-judgemental.

Technique Five: Visualization Meditation

This relaxation technique is a unique take on traditional meditation which aims to bring your attention not only to your vision but to your other four senses as well. Visualization meditation or guided imagery works through envisioning an environment where you find yourself at peace and thus able to release feelings of anxiety or tension.

The setting you choose can be as individualized as you are. It can be a location from your childhood, a sunny beach, or a serene forest. Visualization can be practiced in silence, or with the aid of calm music or even a therapist's voice. To heighten the experience try pairing your visualization with a soundtrack that matches your chosen setting.

Visualization meditation should be practiced in a silent location where you are able to relax and avoid any kind of distractions. To begin, close your eyes and try to picture a peaceful scene. Allow your worries to fade as you transition deeper into this place; imagine as many details as possible. How does this environment smell, sound, or feel?

For the most effective practice, include as much sensory detail as you can. Ideally, this will involve a minimum of three senses. Use an image that truly reflects your own vision of relaxation and peace. Another individual's image will not be as effective as your own. Shape your vision to suit your own desires.

To get a little practice at building your visualization, let's explore a wooden dock on a serene lake.

- Picture yourself walking along the dock. Note all the colors and textures that you see.

- Make observations with each of your senses. What do you hear, see, smell, feel, or taste?

- Imagine the way your vision changes as the sun sets across the water.

- Listen to the birds chirping in the background.

- Allow yourself to feel the coolness of the water as you step in with your bare feet.

- Note the taste of the fresh air.

Welcome the sensations of complete relaxation as you drift into and explore your calming locale. Spend as much time as you would like in that space before opening your eyes and returning to the present moment.

It is perfectly normal to lose track of time or zone out during one of these imagery sessions. If you are concerned with losing time, you can set a timer to ring at a certain interval to remind yourself when it is time to bring your practice to a close. Some individuals will also experience stiff limbs, small muscle movements, or yawning. All of the side effects are perfectly natural.

EXERCISE NINE

Try to remember a place or time where your mind was completely relaxed or at peace. If you can't think of such a time, imagine a place where this would occur.

Now, bringing that image and that place into your mind, start to close your eyes and focus on the details of that place. Use the steps described in *Visualization Meditation* to take this further.

Technique Six: Yoga and Tai Chi

Yoga and Tai Chi are similar relaxation techniques in the sense that they involve specific movements paired with breath work and deep concentration.

While it is impossible to cover all the variations and styles of both Yoga and Tai Chi in this short guide it's worthwhile understanding that performed in the right way both can be a powerful boost to your body and mind.

Most people see arts like Yoga, Pilates or Tai Chi as purely physical endeavors, and they are great for your body in this regard, but the correct forms practiced in a mindful way can be also just as beneficial for the mind as traditional seated meditation.

Yoga

In yoga you will find a series of postures, some stationary and others dynamic. Not only will a dedicated yoga practice bring relaxation, practitioners also find increased strength, flexibility, stamina, and balance. Individuals who practice yoga on a regular basis report greater access to the relaxation response in everyday scenarios. Beginners should seek classes where a trained instructor can lead you through each posture, decreasing the risk of injury.

You might be surprised to learn that there are many forms of yoga to choose from. Nearly every class will include some time spent in a relaxation pose. To maximize the relaxation response choose a form which is slow, and gentle, that involves primarily steady movements paired with deep breathing and gentle stretches. If you are uncertain which form of yoga is right for you, consider asking an instructor at the closest studio. Below is a little information on the most popular yoga forms.

Satyananda Yoga: A form of traditional yoga which is characterized by complete relaxation, gentle poses, and meditation. This form is great for beginners or anyone in search of reduced stress levels.

Hatha Yoga: This common form of yoga is also gentle enough for beginners. Similar to Satyananda yoga, it offers stress relief.

Power Yoga: This form, sometimes also known as Ashtanga, is more stimulating than it is relaxing. It is characterized by intense poses with the goal of obtained superior fitness levels.

Tai Chi

Have you ever witnessed a gathering of people in the park, making slow, synchronized movements? What you happened upon was likely Tai Chi. This style involves slow, flowing movements practiced at your own pace, free of competition. The relaxing movements require great concentration and awareness of your vital energy as it circulates through your body.

Although Tai Chi began as a form of martial arts, it is now often practiced as a means of quieting the mind, strengthening the body, and reducing stress. Like in meditation, individuals will focus on their breath during Tai Chi as a means for remaining grounded in the moment.

As with Yoga, there are a number of variations of traditional Tai Chi ranging from the physically intense and exhausting to the slow and gentle.

This form of relaxation is considered a safe, low-impact activity which suits individuals of all ages and fitness levels. As with yoga, Tai Chi can be performed alone or in a group according to your own personal preference.

Tai Chi is also known as Tai Chi Chuan (Quan) and Yang style Tai Chi is the most commonly practiced style worldwide. (Though of course, it's worth investigating the style that suits you best).

Qi Gong (Chi Gong)

Chi Gong has similar roots to Tai Chi, with connections to traditional Chinese Martial Arts. The term itself relates to "Energy Cultivation".

Although less common in the west, Chi Gong practice is an effective form of mindfulness emphasizing correct posture and careful breathing in a similar way to both Tai Chi and Yoga, but with a focus on visualizing energy throughout the body.

EXERCISE TEN

Yoga, Tai Chi and Chi Gong are all amazing ways to help focus and relax your mind but to truly learn the skills involved a little instruction can be beneficial.

Take a look online an search for Tai Chi classes in your area. Note down the style they practice (there are several) the location and the cost. Next repeat this exercise for Yoga and Pilates classes. These are much more common and you should find a number of local results. Again though, note down the style, distance and cost.

Finally, once you have ten or more options, narrow it down to three that fit you best and get in touch. Most offer a free trial class and if not you are usually welcome to come along and observe without paying. Group exercises are a fantastic way to get involved.

If you can't find any classes nearby or you wish to try before attending any, find the three styles that appeal most to you and take a couple of minutes to watch videos of the techniques online – try the exercises and see how they feel.

Technique Seven: Rhythmic Exercise

To ensure a dedicated practice of your chosen relaxation techniques, you will want to give them a place in your daily routine. Modern life can be hectic between juggling, work, family, school, and other kinds of commitments. Because of this, it is common to find yourself at the end of the day without any to spare for your practicing relaxation. Instead, get creative and discover ways to perform relaxation techniques while you are doing other activities.

Activities which can be classified as *rhythmic exercises*, like cycling, walking, rowing, or running can be effective stress relief tools when practiced with the right state of mind. This works similar to meditation, by engaging your body mindfully in the present. In doing this you will tune in to how your body is feeling right now in this moment.

Perform your chosen exercise while focusing on every movement your body makes, as well as the way your breathing aids each movement. As you notice your mind straying, gently guide the focus back towards the present. Note the sensations you experience through each step or rotation including the way your foot feels as it contacts the ground. Pay attention to the rhythm of each breath and the wind or sun as it caresses your face.

Mindfulness, of you and your surroundings, forms the core of most meditation approaches and is especially applicable here while undertaking your chosen exercise.

EXERCISE ELEVEN

Exercise is an important part of beating stress, even without the meditation practice included. Regular activity increases blood flow, strengthens the heart, releases endorphins and makes you feel good!

If you don't exercise regularly now, try to introduce a small change, including twenty minutes of brisk walking into your daily routine. This is a perfect starting point for improving body and mind.

Once you are either walking, running, swimming or whatever rhythmic exercise you prefer, on a regular basis, bring your attention to the rhythm and movement of your body for two minutes at a time.

Incorporating Relaxation Techniques into Everyday Life

Schedule: Whenever possible schedule your practice into each day by setting aside specific time periods to practice. It can be easier to stick to your schedule if you plan on practicing your techniques in the morning before other commitments have a chance to get in your way.

Multitask: Try practicing your relaxation techniques while you are also doing other things. Consider meditating on the bus or train during a commute, or white seating in a waiting room. Practice deep breathing at home while you fold laundry, vacuum, or mow the lawn. Walking the dog is another great opportunity, or schedule some Tai Chi or yoga during your lunch break.

Mindful Exercise: Improve the relaxation benefits of any exercise routine by adding mindfulness to your workout. Shift your focus to your body during each movement instead of watching the television or listening to music. During resistance training coordinate each breath with each contraction and relaxation. Notice how your muscle feels as you raise and lower the weight.

Choose Alert Moments: Your relaxation attempts won't be as effective if you practice when you are sleepy. In fact, you will simply be more likely to fall asleep. Try to choose times when you are awake and alert. You will also want to wait a while after a big meal and avoid using drug, tobacco, or alcohol.

Prepare for Challenges: It won't always be easy to fit relaxation techniques into your day. Some days you might just not feel like doing it. Be ready to fight to find the motivation sometimes. Remember that your efforts will be rewarded by the pleasant relaxation response and long-term benefits. If you do happen to skip a day or even several weeks, don't give up altogether. It can take a while before these practices become routine, so jump right back in as soon as you can.

Breath Work

Meditation can be performed in numerous ways, and many of those may seem to conflict with one another. Some will instruct you to keep your eyes closed while others suggest they remain open. Meanwhile one may suggest you chose a focal point or listen to music when another recommends you sit in silence, focusing on nothing in particular. In the end, there is no wrong way to meditate. Whatever choices help you arrive at a relaxed state of mind are the right ones. The one factor that unites meditation techniques is the practice of paying attention to and controlling your breath.

Within the classic text, *The Miracle of Mindfulness*, Thich Nhat Hanh describes the ways in which your breath is connected to your mind which in turn controls the body. Becoming attentive to your breath, and thus making it more fluid, can lead the entire body and mind to a place of stillness. Practicing meditation will teach an individual's mind how to become more fully engaged in the moment.

With our minds pulled in so many directions accomplishing this can be quite a challenge. You begin to breathe in and out, only to suddenly remember something you needed to do today. One way to deal with this distraction is to try counting your breaths rather than simply following them. Inhale and count one, exhale and count one. Inhale a second time and count two, exhale a second time and count two. Continue through this pattern until you complete the tenth cycle then begin again.

Counting in this way forces your mind to focus on your breath. If you are not mindful during your practice you will no doubt lose count and need to begin again. With more practice though, you will get better at focusing your mind on the task at hand.

Nhat Hanh believed that this skill has many more applications besides the stolen moments of meditation. Indeed, it can be quiet helpful in moments of stress, when you need to do something you are uncomfortable with, such as making a public speech or when you find yourself overwhelmed with the volume of work before you.

Mantras

The term mantra can be translated to the phrase, "that which protects the mind". Repeating a mantra is said to provide protection in the form of spiritual power. As you speak a mantra, you charge your breath through the energy which resides within that mantra.

When you choose your own mantra, try to find a word or phrase that has meaning in your life. Mantras can be found in many spiritual traditions. For examples, Catholics recite the Rosary, while the Buddhists of Tibet recite words of peace, healing, and spiritual transformation. "Live peace", "relax", and "I am strong" are a few good mantras.

Guided Meditations

A guided meditation is similar in many ways to guided imagery. Both are effective techniques which help to focus the mind and engage in an imagined scenario with real benefits. Choose a guided meditation which feels both simple and authentic. You can practice at home with an audio recording, or join a meditation class where an instructor will guide your mind.

Some guided meditations are practiced with specific goals in mind. Some are designed to ease insomnia or conquer fears. You may also find 10 or 15-minute mini guided meditations which are great when you need to squeeze your practice into a lunch or coffee break. Although no meditation can guarantee results, they do offer an opportunity to strengthen your focus and discover a sense of peace, when practiced regularly. The only downside is that you can become reliant on another for the guidance.

Buddhist Meditation

Buddhism holds a number of unique meditation traditions. Despite their differences, all of these techniques hold several similarities. One of the similarities is known as shikantaza.

Shikantaza is the practice of "just sitting". Here the individual dulls their senses, allowing the mind to become quiet. The practitioner is seated on a rounded cushion (a Zafu), with their legs folded. In this position, the spine is elevated just above your knees. It is important to sit tall, without leaning in any particular direction. The head too is held high without tipping. One aspect the observer may not notice is the tongue which is held against the back of the upper teeth.

Alternative sitting positions involve seiza, or kneeling, and seiza bench, which implements a short bench which helps to raise the practitioner's hips. Individuals with physical limitations are permitted to sit in a chair.

The explanations for each of these elements are vague. Still, these kinds of positions do hold practical benefits. Holding the tongue in the described position calms the swallowing reflex and relaxes the jaw, eliminating that particular distraction.

In Buddhist meditation, the eyes are held half-open and posed downward 45 degrees in a relaxed manner. Your left hand is cupped inside the right hand with the thumbs gently touching so as to form a circle. The forearms rest upon the thighs.

Although this posture may seem awkward in the beginning, most practitioners find it becomes quite natural over time. It is a very stable arrangement, providing relaxation without the threat of tumbling over. Many Buddhist meditations are traditionally practiced facing a wall, to limit potential distractions. Still, other methods are performed facing another individual, a teacher, or an altar.

Like many of the relaxation techniques previously discussed, Buddhist meditation requires a quiet environment, free of distractions. The space you choose should be neither dark or light, hot nor cold. It is important to avoid shifting around, scratching itches, or stretching muscles, as this may prove distracting other individuals who are also trying to focus on their meditation. Focusing your mind will allow these urges to simply melt away.

Here there is a goal of withdrawing the senses as well as the mind's busy thoughts. Instead, the goal is to simply sit, with the mind relaxed, but without falling asleep. Therefore it is necessary to let go of daydreams, planning, or reminiscing, and sit in silence. While it sounds simple, this task can take time and dedication to master. In addition to being straightforward, this practice can be truly profound.

"There are techniques of Buddhism, such as meditation, that anyone can adopt."

- *Dalai Lama*

What is 'Zen'?

As a term, Zen has come to mean a number of different things depending on the context and which part of the world you are from. Indeed it often includes statements that seem contradictory to the outsider. This nebulous concept makes it hard to give a specific definition for everyone but there are elements you can take from it even as a casual observer.

In the west 'Zen' is often applied to individuals or characteristics of a peaceful and unhindered nature. One who is calm and leading a positive life is often known as being 'zen' in their attitude.

"Dave didn't let the situation bother him, he was so zen."

This approach is often seen as an enviable trait and something to aspire to.

But this is a slightly deviated version of the original school of Zen Buddhism where the term originated.

Zen, as a form of Buddhism, originated in the East during the 6th Century. Although thought to begin in China, the philosophy soon moved to Vietnam, Korea and, perhaps most famously, Japan.

Zen Buddhism has a slightly different focus to the many other traditional forms. Instead of developing a textbook understanding of the sutras or religious doctrine (as in many religions) it emphasizes the personal aspect of understanding. I.E - your own personal insights into Buddhism, primarily through the direct experience of Meditation.

In this regard, it is focused on the now and the singular moment of experience, rather than looking forward, back and all around for enlightenment.

Even the term 'Zen' is thought to approximate to Meditative state or Meditation when translated from the earliest texts to the modern tongue.

So what does this mean to me?

As a general term of peaceful and positive being, 'Zen' in the west is an ideal to strive towards that demonstrates an easier way of living. This can mean you are more conscious of your emotions and generally more calm and aware of your outlook as you embrace others and the world around you.

In many ways it can become a Mantra, a phrase you use to remind yourself of the attitude you would like to have; being 'Zen'

While the colloquial Zen approach is fairly straightforward, the intricate philosophies of Zen Buddhism might be a little harder for the average person on the street to understand. The simplest lesson to take from it all is one of being in the moment. Something echoed through most of the meditation practices you will find.

We spend too long planning, thinking and being bombarded by information every hour of the day.

Try to develop a simple awareness of what you are doing, and how you feel right now without judgment.

Instead of wondering what if, what could be and what was. Just be.

ASMR: The Zen Sensation

What is it?

ASMR stands for Autonomous Sensory Meridian Response. The term Autonomous implies that the response can be triggered at will. ASMR is a pleasant physical sensation, originating at the top of the head region and sometimes traveling down the spine or limbs. It is often described as a natural high. Some people believe it can be applied as a cure for insomnia and other stress-related issues.

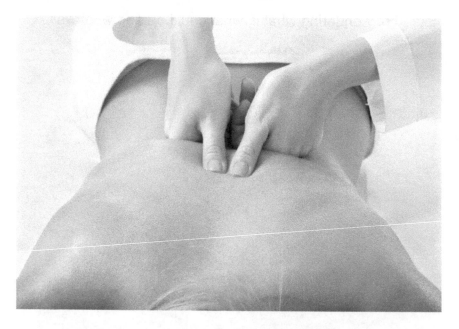

Since ASMR has just recently come under awareness there have not yet been any documented scientific studies. Therefore, the information available is small and limited to descriptions of individual experiences.

The extent to which ASMR is now being reported suggests that this is something that people have likely experienced throughout history, but kept private. Now in the age of the internet little is kept private anymore. There are discussion boards on nearly every topic, ASMR being one. As individuals began to discuss their experiences, many commonalities were found.

Many individuals with ASMR experiences describe the response as a state of enlightenment. In this way, ASMR is similar to meditation. Another similarity is the "zoned out" state of mind which can be likened to a meditative state where an individual withdraws from their environment to focus internally. Perhaps ASMR is touching the experience of a higher level of human consciousness.

How it Feels:

Experiencing an ASMR episode is a tremendously personal and can be difficult to describe. In general, it might be defined as a pleasant kind headache which radiates down through your spine. Sometimes it might also radiate across your shoulders and down your arms or legs.

ASMR is quite similar to a meditative state where the individual approaches a moment of bliss free of stress or anxiety. One of the more concrete analogies is to imagine a scalp massage, but the tingling happens inside of your head. It is commonly paired with a trance-like state where you withdraw from your surroundings.

What Causes it?

Research is needed to determine the cause of ASMR. This would involve a diagnostic tool such as a functional MRI which would help determine what is happening at the chemical level. Discovering which chemicals are involved in the process might aid in explaining why the response "feels good" to most individuals.

Some theorize that the response can be traced to childhood, suggesting that an individual's awareness of ASMR may be related to how they were treated by their parents. This may prove to have some validity as most individuals who experience ASMR report their first encounters as happening during early childhood. A kind, gentle touch also seems to be one of the big triggers for ASMR. These triggers which are commonly divided into Type A, internal stimuli, and Type B external stimuli. Many involve slow-paced, deliberate actions or sounds.

Common Triggers:

- Listening to lectures, instructional videos, talk radio, or unique speech patterns
- Art or Music
- Witnessing someone work on a task which requires concentration.
- Attention from another individual.
- Getting or watching a haircut or massage
- Listening to someone whisper or speak a foreign language
- Being tickled
- Repetitive noises such as a dripping faucet, tapping on a keyboard, or a bouncing ball
- Feeling someone draw on your skin
- Watching a person use sign language
- Listening to a stranger or an elderly individual speak with a relaxing voice
- Reading an engaging book, newspaper, or pamphlet
- Teaching someone a new skill
- Witnessing someone trim or file their nails

Side Effects

Since ASMR can be a very pleasant and relaxing experience, some individuals report feeling very tired after an episode. Others may find themselves feeling sad, possibly even shedding a tear or two.

Some people have odd visual occurrences, particularly if they close their eyes. The main negative side effects reported so far involve slight headaches, nausea, and fatigue. A few individuals have also reported a disruption to their ability to focus on the task at hand, likely because their attention is drawn to a more internal, personal experience.

The Biggest Meditation Mistake (For Most People)

What Next?

It's easy when we start a new activity to get very excited at the start and then quickly tail off and quit when we grow accustomed to it.

From a scientific level, it comes down to the way our brain works with pleasure-inducing hormones and their appropriate receivers. A small amount stimulates a positive response but over-do it and the mind becomes dulled to the pleasurable sensation.

Perhaps the most famous example is that of drug abusers. Initially, only a small amount is required for the 'high' but over time more and more is needed.

It's a similar, though far more positive process when we undertake Meditation.

Starting out we are full of enthusiasm and upon perfecting a certain technique we find the relaxation and mindful response pleasurable and easy to achieve. But then a thought arises:

"Now what?"

In the modern world we are programmed to look for linear progression and as such we expect meditation to continue in an upward slope; increased effort for the increased reward.

But it doesn't work like that. Meditation works best as part of a steady daily practice that doesn't necessarily increase in duration or effort.

So it's quite common to find that after a couple of months of daily 2, 3 or 10-minute meditation your mind starts to wander and the pleasurable sensation starts to wane.

This is the key moment

For many people, once they start to see fewer results they simply quit. This is fine if, say you are on a weight loss programme and achieve your desired weight, but in something like Meditation it is a long-term practice that delivers the best results.

So when you start to feel like you are losing that focus there are two approaches to get you back on track.

Reduce the duration

Or

Change the Technique

Reducing duration

If after establishing a daily routine including meditation you have increased your peaceful time beyond the original 2 Minutes (and this is quite natural), then any time you start to feel less enthusiastic or pushed for time simply reduce the time to the original 2 Minutes and start again.

There is no judgment, no penalty for doing less time. Remember that mediation is not a race to some goal. The journey, the experience is what matters.

You can always drop the time back to that original 2 minutes any time you feel like it and extend it from there. Or stay at the 2 Minutes, depending on how you feel. It is, after all completely personal.

Changing Techniques

The other approach relies on tricking your brain to re-engage interest and the pleasure receptors.

In the simplest form, if you have been using one method for your chosen Meditation E.g. Deep Breathing (Technique one in this guide) then switch to another technique, (say Visualisation – Technique Five), and continue using this instead.

The change of approach and new exercise should re-energize you and increase motivation. This can be completed any time you find yourself drifting from daily practice.

You can also combine reduced duration and change technique to really refresh your practice and prevent any complacency.

Give it a go!

EXERCISE TWELVE

This one is easy. If you have established a meditation practice and you find yourself missing days out or skipping the odd session, refer back to The Biggest Meditation Mistake section and go back to basics.

Remember that meditation is a journey, not a destination. The benefits come from taking a small amount of action every day and enjoying the process.

Quick Tips and Tricks

The following are some quick ideas to boost your ability to meditate and help keep a regular routine.

1. Tell People

Quite often it's very easy to skip a session or forget about a meditation practice if we are the only ones that know about it.

Tell your friends, family, co-workers and anyone you think may remind you. Not only will it make it harder to forget but it will also encourage you to stick to a regular schedule when people are asking you about it!

2. The Calendar Method

Buy one of those traditional calendars with a box for each day in the month. For every day you complete your 2 Minutes of Meditation (Or longer) mark the box with an 'X'.

As the days build up you will gradually fill up the month, creating a pattern on the chart. This has the strangely powerful effect of creating a chain of visible 'X's which you will never want to break!

(Writers have used this technique for many years)

3. Use a Timer Application

Most people operate a cell or mobile phone these days. Much of the time they are simply stress inducing distractions in our life, never allowing us to fully switch off.

Time to make them useful!

Depending on your phone you will typically find there are thousands of 'Apps' (Applications) available for download. Many of them free.

Grab a simple timer or stopwatch App, set it for 2 minutes and let it tell you when the time is up. This way you can fully focus on the task at hand and ignore any thoughts of duration.

Even if you don't use mobile apps, traditional timers can be used in the same way.

4. Get Comfy

Everyone has different flexibility levels. Don't force yourself into a position that hurts. One thing that can help you is a cushion, specifically one designed for meditation. These help you achieve good posture and easier relaxation. (See the Meditation Cushions section).

Exercises

If you've made it this far and not yet tried any of the exercises in this guide, now is the time to get started. You don't have to complete them all in one go, but taking even a small amount of action is an important step to developing a meditation habit that sticks with you for life.

Below is a summary of the exercises listed throughout this book:

EXERCISE ONE:

Set a timer on your phone or computer for two minutes, with an alarm at the end. Start the countdown and then go back to whatever you were doing in your daily life. Don't look at the timer.

Whether you were at work, on the computer or out walking—whatever you were up to I guarantee that the alarm will go off quicker than expected. Two minutes feels like nothing at all.

Still feel like you don't have the time to spare?

EXERCISE TWO:

What do you want to achieve from meditation? There is no right or wrong answer to this question but you do need to think about it.

Take a notepad or create a note on your phone and write down:

- Three things that stress you out on a regular basis

- Three ways you would like to improve this
- Three things you would like to get from meditation – your goals.

EXERCISE THREE:

Write down a list of all the things you think you need to get started in meditation. Done? Good, now eliminate all but three of those things, focusing purely on the most important ones. Be brutally honest and zero in on the ones you require, not the ones you want.

You now have a list of the things you *really* need.

EXERCISE FOUR:

Make a note of which times of the day you are running around like a crazy person, and which times you are most at peace. Find a point where you have your own time and space and where you are neither fully stressed or fully relaxed.

For many this will be after the initial morning dash to work or school but before they relax for the evening. A point around lunchtime or mid-morning can work well.

This will be your ideal starting point.

EXERCISE FIVE

Find a quiet place and take a seat. Straighten your back, open your chest and try the *Deep Breathing Meditation* process listed, for just two minutes.

Initially, don't worry about taking the process further or reaching some higher state of consciousness. Just be present and breathe.

EXERCISE SIX

It's incredibly easy for us to hold tension in our bodies without realizing it. For this exercise, we will find that tension and gently release it.

When you are next at home, find a space where you can lie down and relax—but not too much—we don't want to fall asleep.

Then, begin the *Progressive Muscle Relaxation* Technique and work down your own body, using the method described. Find, recognize and release tension along the way.

EXERCISE SEVEN

Starting in the same way as the previous exercise, find a space where you can fully stretch out and relax.

Then, take a couple of minutes to bring the attention to the bottom of your feet and work your way up the body using the Body Scan Technique described. Once again, find and release tension along the way.

EXERCISE EIGHT

Mindfulness is one of the most powerful meditation exercises available, so if you try only one method, make it this one.

Start by sitting in a relaxed but upright position and breathe in and out slowly, then focus your mind and follow the *Mindfulness* process, being present and non-judgemental.

EXERCISE NINE

Try to remember a place or time where your mind was completely relaxed or at peace. If you can't think of such a time, imagine a place where this would occur.

Now, bringing that image and that place into your mind, start to close your eyes and focus on the details of that place. Use the steps described in *Visualization Meditation* to take this further.

EXERCISE TEN

Yoga, Tai Chi and Chi Gong are all amazing ways to help focus and relax your mind but to truly learn the skills involved a little instruction can be beneficial.

Take a look online and search for Tai Chi classes in your area. Note down the style they practice (there are several) the location and the cost. Next repeat this exercise for Yoga and Pilates classes. These are much more common and you should find a number of local results. Again though, note down the style, distance and cost.

Finally, once you have ten or more options, narrow it down to three that fit you best and get in touch. Most offer a free trial class and if not you are usually welcome to come along and observe without paying. Group exercises are a fantastic way to get involved.

If you can't find any classes nearby or you wish to try before attending any, find the three styles that appeal most to you and take a couple of minutes to watch videos of the techniques online – try the exercises and see how they feel.

EXERCISE ELEVEN

Exercise is an important part of beating stress, even without the meditation practice included. Regular activity increases blood flow, strengthens the heart, releases endorphins and makes you feel good!

If you don't exercise regularly now, try to introduce a small change, including twenty minutes of brisk walking into your daily routine. This is a perfect starting point for improving body and mind.

Once you are either walking, running, swimming or whatever rhythmic exercise you prefer, on a regular basis, bring your attention to the rhythm and movement of your body for two minutes at a time.

EXERCISE TWELVE

This one is easy. If you have established a meditation practice and you find yourself missing days out or skipping the odd session, refer back to The Biggest Meditation Mistake section and go back to basics.

Remember that meditation is a journey, not a destination. The benefits come from taking a small amount of action every day and enjoying the process.

Thank you for reading.

Thank you for reading, I hope you enjoyed this book and it helps you toward a healthier, more relaxed life.

I'm an independent author creating guides to inspire and help people in the best way I can, but I don't have a publisher's backing like many big names. I always appreciate your feedback, so please give this book 5 stars if you found it useful!

If you'd like to discover more about how to develop the power of your mind and how to unlock your inner potential, be sure to check out my bestselling book; Mental Combat.

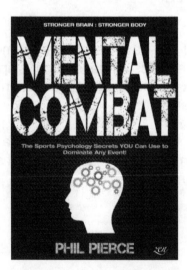

http://getbook.at/MentalCombat

- *Phil*

Recommended Reads:

There are a number of excellent Books on Meditation out there. If you are interested in furthering your practice and perhaps discovering more on the capabilities of your mind, check out:

How to Meditate: A Practical Guide to Making Friends with Your Mind – Pema Chodron

http://www.amazon.com/How-Meditate-Practical-Friends-ebook/dp/B00C2BYPMY

The Miracle of Mindfulness: An Introduction to the Practice of Meditation – Thich Nhat Hanh

http://www.amazon.com/The-Miracle-Mindfulness-Introduction-ebook/dp/B009U9S6VM

Copyright:

CPSIA information can be obtained
at www.ICGtesting.com
Printed in the USA
LVHW02s2339100918
589768LV00008B/230/P